This book is dedicated to you, the reader.

CONTENTS

INTRO

I couldn't believe it. My heart was racing, my nerves were flip-flopping in my stomach. At twelve years of age, I found myself standing backstage at the Sydney Opera House, getting ready to compete in a poetry slam off in front of hundreds of people, as well as media and one of my poetry idols.

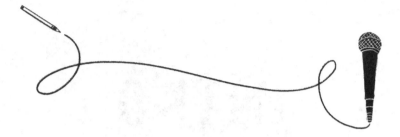

Hi, I'm Solli (which you might have guessed from reading the cover). I'm a poet, performer, and now, an author.

WHHHHHOOOOOOOHHHHHOOOOOOOO!!!!!!

I have always dreamed of becoming an author, but I didn't think it would happen before I was an adult! I'm so lucky to be sharing my journey because maybe this book will help you to dream big too.

So let me tell you a bit more about myself before I get back to how I ended up on that amazing Opera House stage.

I love writing, playing tennis and table tennis, and creating music—I play the saxophone, keyboard, and drums. I compete in long-distance running events, and love training for them … especially when there's an event coming up, then I'm like, "oh man, I gotta start training hard for that!"

This book is something I started to write when I was thinking of becoming a slam poet. Basically, I wanted to encourage others to create poetry and also talk about some of the issues I think are important for my generation. I love helping people be the best that they can be, and I'm truly passionate about the types of changes that can make tomorrow better than today! That idea in itself is my motivation for doing what I do.

And over the past year I've realized that by writing this book, I might be able to help people like you to become a slam poet.

Some people like going to slams as a form of meaningful entertainment. This is because slam poets usually use their personal experience to tell a poetic story. Sometimes a slam poet will focus their work on a topic that they want to raise awareness of. Like me—I'm passionate about discussing humanitarianism and the environment, along with several other important issues. By becoming a slam poet, you can be a voice for your generation and talk about issues that matter most to you. Plus, becoming a slam poet is a fun experience!

Poetry often features rhymes, and my first

memory of rhyming is having Dr. Seuss books read to me every night, for years and years—and years. My mum loves to rhyme and it's something we've always done around the house. Most of my family has a love of poetry and rhyme too.

In my early primary school years, I found myself writing narratives in poetic verse in school and after school as a hobby. I have no idea how this happened … it was just what I liked to do. (I used to imagine that my comics written in a poetic style would one day become as famous as *The Simpsons*. Keep dreaming! … I know, right?)

I was nine when I learned my first technical style of poetry, the haiku. (You can read a haiku and many more of the poems I've written in Part 2 of the book.) From then on, the wonderful world of poetry opened up to me.

After finishing primary school in 2016, I started homeschooling for my high school education, which gave me time to learn more about poetry. I wrote poems frequently and found a love for different technical styles, and my favorite style— slam poetry. My mum showed me YouTube clips of some rappers and a slam poet, and that was when I knew I was going to become a slam poet. I was hooked.

When I was in our local library only a few months later, I found a brochure that read:

Coffs Harbour Heat—Australian Poetry
Slam 2017 on the 24th of August.

My mum said she was going to enter. (Wait! Before I continue, you must know that one thing I love more than slam poetry is trying to beat my mum at pretty much everything!!)

So, I raced home to think about what I should write and that's when I wrote my first piece, "Evolution." After three weeks of writing, typing, and reciting, it was time for the local poetry slam heats. While battling with EXTREME nerves and excitement, and—of course—performing my poem, I won!

This was a complete surprise. It was only my first poetry slam, and I was also doing it as part of my homework for English.

Long story short, after six weeks of sporadic writer's block, more EXTREME nerves, excitement, and then travelling to Sydney, it was time for the state finals held at the State Library of New South Wales. This is where I first recited my "Australian Air" poem.

The competition at the state final was fierce, with some really creative entrants—poet after poet. And I came second!

What????

Yes, I came second by *one-tenth* of a point.

That meant I was off to the Sydney Opera House for the Australian national finals!

Twenty-four hours later, I was backstage at the Sydney Opera House—let me repeat—the Sydney Opera House! It was amazing! The architectural design of the building is truly something, and the stage was massive. I've never seen anything like it.

The way the event worked was that competitors' names were randomly drawn out of a hat, so I didn't know when I'd be called to the stage. (Scary, right?) So, after two rounds, where I recited "Australian Air" and "Embrace Our Differences," it was me and one other person left in the competition. That meant a tie—an equal score, and a SLAM OFF!!!!!

Luckily, I had one last poem, "Evolution." This was it, and I knew that I really had to give it my all—everything!

Moments later, I WON!!!!

My heart's pounding right now as I write this, with the memories rushing back … I had won the national final and the title of 2017–18 Australian Poetry Slam Champion, against all adult competitors, and I was only 12 years of age. I still can't even get my head around this! It was a wonderful feeling having the audience cheer loudly for me, especially at the Sydney Opera House.

Since then I've been really busy, with radio

interviews, TV appearances, and racing around the country for poetry performances, gigs, and private events.

This opportunity = 100% AWESOME!!!

In that time, I also finished off the book you're currently reading and squeezed in my schooling.

Looking back, it was worth the nerves and overcoming the stage fright I felt. I can now perform in front of thousands of people with fewer nerves than I had performing in front of those original 50 people at the local poetry slam heats. And I get to share my poetry with you all.

I've had an amazing time on my journey to becoming a slam poet, and you will too. So, get comfy, sit back, and enjoy learning how to read and write poetry, and get ready to walk onto that stage.

And into the LIMELIGHT ...

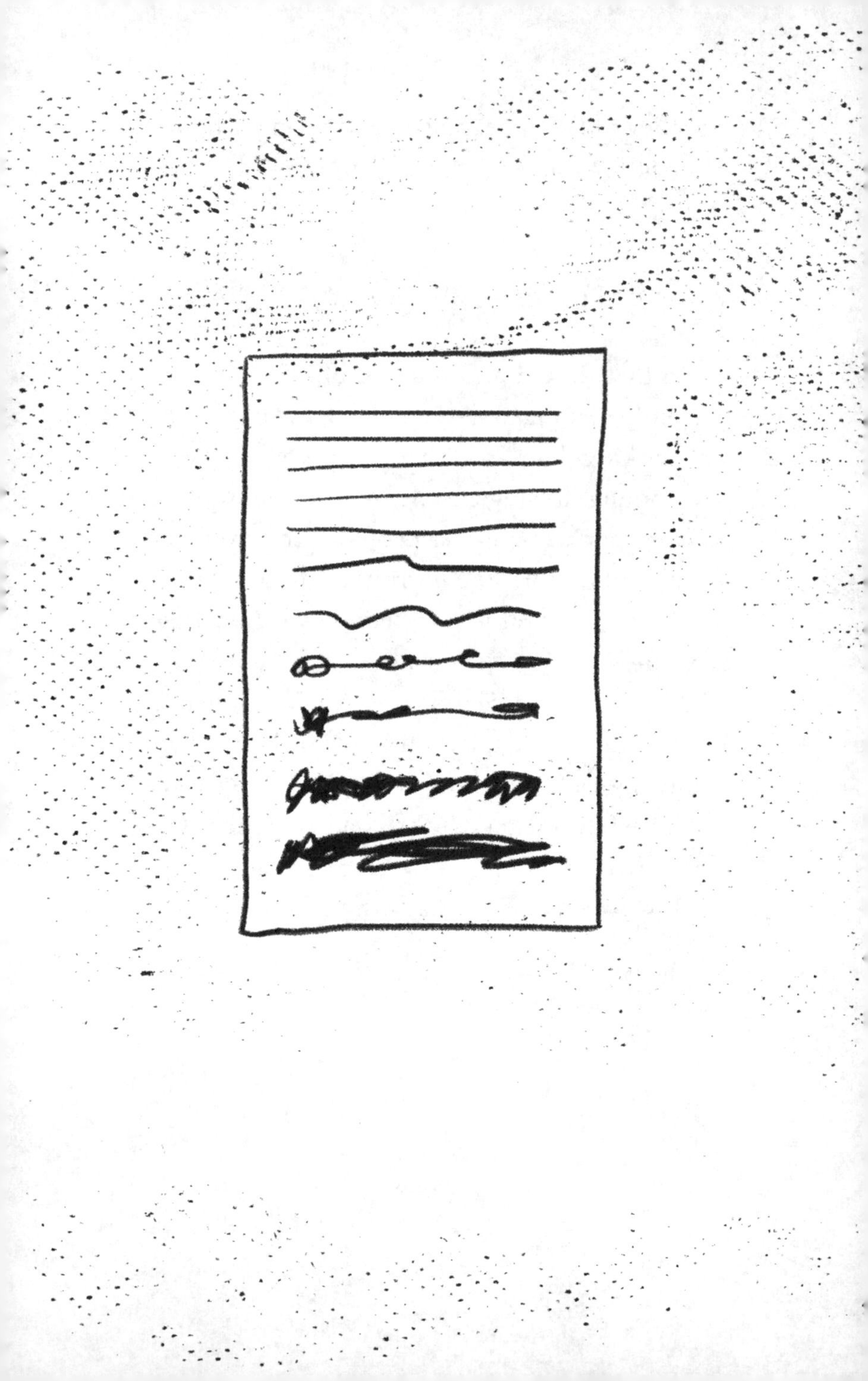

chapter 1
POETRY

poetry (noun)

1. A literary art form that uses words to describe a theme or topic, or to tell a story in a creative style.

2. A rhyme.

Poetry is much more than a bunch of words. Poetry is rhythm and flow, meter and rhyme, sentiment and strategy.

Fierce rap battles and intriguing slam poetry performances on YouTube made up my first Year 7 poetry lesson. My teacher (aka my mum) helped me to understand modern poetry as well as traditional forms, and it was interesting to learn where my style of writing could fit in (although I don't think any of us should compare our talents or our skills to one another's ... we just need to be the best version of ourselves). When I watched the clips, I was amazed by the art of slam poetry. It seemed crazy-fun and interesting because of how many different topics were raised in the poems, and I just found that slam poetry was really like how I usually write.

From here, my passion for slam poetry grew even bigger. I started following many great slam artists like Omar Musa, Harry Baker, Luka Lesson, and Ian Keteku—who is the poetry idol I mentioned in the intro. This helped me to reflect on my own style of writing. Combining my English lessons with reading books on traditional poetry and researching poetry, I learned that poetry has a rich history.

I think poems are like stories being told in really creative ways. Poetry offers a combination of images, feelings, and experiences, often influential or sentimental, which means sometimes when I write a poem I express what I think or feel, and other times I want the audience to think/feel these things too.

When I started writing the poem "Game Changer" (which I performed at the Adelaide Fringe Festival in South Australia), I had it in my mind that it was going to be about me. I don't mean that in a selfish way, but I wanted to influence how people live by offering ideas on an environmentally friendly lifestyle and encouraging them to help others within their community. But as I wrote the poem, I felt it was more a representation of my generation. Many of us, like you and me, are trying our hardest to make changes to help our future be better.

The serious part of poetry is the technical bits, like how a poem is constructed using themes, stanzas, verses, and lines. And this takes some time to absorb. Traditionally, some cultures pass on poetry through theater and songs, but the first ever poem written down was probably carved into stone. Wow! I'm happy that technology has advanced since then because I would still be carving my first poem if it wasn't for computers, pens, and paper!

Through my poetry journey, I've learned about a lot of different poetry styles. Each usually has a set of rules or ideas that determine how the specific structure should be written. For example, a villanelle is a 19-line poem that is made up of five three-line stanzas and the sixth stanza has four lines, known as a quatrain. Confused? It probably helps to read a poem in the villanelle style to understand how it's constructed. (There's one in Part 2 called "The Places You Can Go With One Idea.") That's how I got to know different forms, by picking them apart and giving it a go writing my own.

Limericks are one of my favorite types of poems to write. They're not complex and they get my creative flow going, so I often write one before I tackle a longer poem, like my slam poetry. Limericks have five lines and are meant to be fun, and funny, and often don't make much sense, so a limerick is really known as a nonsense poem. The first, second, and fifth lines rhyme, and they have eight or nine syllables, while the third and fourth lines rhyme, and they have five or six syllables. The first sentence often starts with: *There once was a* ... and then flows on from there. Check out one of my limericks, "After Lunch," in the collection at the back of this book.

At the beginning of Year 7, I started learning Spanish. Studying words, sounds, and sentence structures of another language is so fascinating. To help me practice, I wrote a poem—in Spanish! It's called "Árbol de Helado" ... I won't say what that translates to, but I can tell you that it's about two things I can't live without. And it's exciting to see if people will be able to pick out any bits of the poem, even if they're not fluent in Spanish ... but I guess that's what poetry is about—interpretation.

So when was the first poem written? No one really knows, but the popularity of poetry has risen and fallen many, many times since people started telling stories thousands of years ago. Haiku, acrostic, ballad, lyric, verse, limerick, sonnet, Shakespearean sonnet, free verse, blank verse, and shape poetry are the most commonly used styles among poets. But the list continues beyond that, so make sure you do your own research to see what types of poetry you like.

While there's a classical tone to the history of poetry, slam poetry is what I'm known for and what I love creating and performing. It offers a lot of freedom in things like the flow, structure, and length of the poem, and performing poetry is what it's all about for me.

chapter 2
SLAM POETRY

slam poetry (noun)

Performance-based poetry that incorporates a variety of topics, emotions, beliefs, and writing styles, often to share a message or to influence a change in an important area of life.

Slam poetry, spoken word poetry, and rap are all different, but what makes these art forms so special is that you use a stack of emotion to express your thoughts to the audience. For me, being able to put words together to create something exceptional that inspires the crowd is the true meaning of slam poetry. I love writing about my feelings and beliefs, mixing in creative ideas and keeping to a certain structure, rhythm, or beat.

While slam poetry has traditionally been the competition form of spoken word poetry, it's slowly being seen as more than that, and now it's kind of like an entertaining performance-based style of poetry. That's what's so amazing about it—the style itself is changing, and in that way, it's also similar to hip-hop.

I'm not a rapper, although I'm sure my neighbors think I am 'cause they can hear me at my keyboard at home—but who cares what people think, yeh? Anyway, hip-hop and rap music are awesome to listen to, especially when you think about how the whole movement originated as a way for people to express themselves. And that has led to other elements of hip-hop culture springing up—beatbox, break dancing, graffiti art.

I reckon that's what could happen to slam poetry too. It could be used in schools as a way to learn about literature, drama, or whatever topics a teacher or student wants. From what I've seen at slam workshops, us kids LOVE learning how to slam— many compare the experience to learning how to rap. It's fun stuff!

Slam poetry is growing in popularity so much that there are now groups and large organizations where people gather weekly or monthly to perform for fun. Sometimes these slam hubs are also held to engage cultural awareness or help develop writing and performance skills within a supportive and non-competitive environment.

A poetry slam event encourages freedom in how a poem is delivered to the audience, as a poem can be spoken, sung, or even rapped out on stage. When you're reading a poem, it's important to understand the rhythm, flow, and stresses, depending on the style of poetry. One of the best things about slam poetry is that the creator controls the speed and rhythm.

Apparently when I was a toddler I would rap along (in toddler language) to the songs my mum listened to on the radio. And when I was about six I would come home from school with a new tongue twister we'd learned in class. I could always recite tongue twisters without any trouble, over and over again, and my mum knew I had a gift for memorizing words at that point. As much as she tried to recite them, she usually ended up laughing, so she just kept her fast-speaking skills for when she was rushing me to get ready for school or tennis lessons. Tongue twisters are a great activity to practice if you want to become a fast-speaking slam poet.

One of the challenges I've set for myself is to learn a new word every day. Sometimes this blows out to a word a week depending on the difficulty of the definition and spelling. But this is probably how my vocabulary has grown a lot over the last couple of years—by exploring the dictionary and thesaurus daily.

When I read about how slam poetry started in the U.S. over 30 years ago, I was amazed that it began with a young construction worker (called Marc Smith) organizing a poetry competition and setting specific rules for the participants. Poets were encouraged to compete against each other within a short time frame, which is still what happens today in poetry slam competitions.

Some people struggle with the idea of poetry competitions because each poem is different and there's no real measure for comparison. That's why the way that a poetry slam event is judged is unique and, I think, fair. Poetry slams are judged by members of the audience, chosen at random. Often the MC throws lollipops out to the audience, and whoever catches a lollipop becomes a judge for that round. New judges are selected for each heat or round.

Poetry slam competitions run by different organizers have slightly different rules, but the main rules common to all are:

- Time limit: often two or three minutes
- Original content: a poem can't have been performed before
- Performance: a work can be performed in any style the poet chooses—spoken word, slam, singing
- Props: sometimes props are allowed

- Judges: randomly selected audience members
- If you win your local heat, you move to the next heat until the final round
- Some comps have a participant limit, so it pays to arrive early if it's first in, best dressed
- Clapping is not allowed and instead the audience clicks their fingers if they like a part of a poem, or the entire poem

Poetry's various styles came from all over the world. For example, the haiku originated in Japan and the lyric poem in Ancient Greece. Every country, time, and culture has had different ways of telling stories through poetry. Perhaps slam poetry is my generation's cultural lingo. I hope it's just the beginning for this powerful style of poetry because it's helped me to share so much with the world already.

chapter 3
IDEAS DON'T GROW ON TREES

write (verb)

To express using words formed on a surface or material.

People often ask how I decide what to write about. Well, I know from experience that ideas don't grow on trees. And sometimes ideas don't come along easily when I want them to. What I've learned to focus on is capturing ideas when they do appear (ha, ha, haaa!—you can't escape from my fingertips now, idea!).

I like to keep pen and paper around the house, in the car, in my schoolbag, and next to my bed for when those awesome ideas spring up. Having easy access to a pen and paper helps to capture that good idea before I forget it. I try to keep a notebook in my pocket and a pencil in my afro because ideas seem to flow best when I write them down by hand, but I use my phone and laptop at times too. And at the end of the day, I transfer my notes/ideas/poems to my journal. I have a lot of journals now and they're part of my everyday life.

BRAINSTORMING

A good way to bring about ideas is to spend some time writing creatively by brainstorming at the same time every day. Just like how some people walk the dog at 7 a.m. every morning or others go to the gym for a 4 p.m. workout, I like to be methodical when it comes to new works. Inspiration can jump out at you anytime, but dedicating time daily helps to grow your inspiration muscles. And when they get strong enough through creative writing training, you'll find it easier to pluck inspiration from anywhere.

With most things, the more you do something, the better you get. And this applies to the creative writing process. The more you write poetry, the better you will get at it!

FIGURATIVE SPEECH

Another method I use to create ideas for my poetry is to pick an item each day of the week and write about it using different methods of figurative speech. I learned about this writing device from my

Year 6 teacher (thanks, Mr. Howard!). Figurative speech is the use of a word or a collection of words to describe something in a creative way. It's one of the main ways to make writing interesting, so without it I don't think many people would read books, magazines, or even newspapers.

Here are some forms of figurative speech I use in my poems:

Simile: Uses the words *like* or *as* to compare nouns, objects, or ideas.

Example: *And it goes through our blood veins, and acts **like** a water main.*

This is more exciting than saying: air is really important and it's called oxygen when it travels through our bodies.

Metaphor: Describes a suggested likeness that isn't a literal meaning of the word or phrase.

Example: *I **am** the lightning that makes thunder— rumble.*

I could have written: my poetry makes people think about what's happening in the world.

Idiom: A word or expression commonly used in a particular country or language that isn't meant literally.

Example: *Thoughts bloom …*

I could have written: we come up with ideas.

Personification: Giving nouns human characteristics.

Example: *Our ice caps are crying.*

I could have written: the ice caps are melting.

Alliteration: This is one of my favorite styles of figurative speech. It's the use of words that start with the same letter and can sometimes have the same sounds too.

Example: *The Tree Trunks' Trust team take some time to talk. To take two minutes to think …*

ACTIVITIES
Blending figurative speech with the topics I like to write about helps to create emotive and interesting poetry. But if you're not used to writing with figurative speech, try these exercises to build up your writing skills. Go on … give it a try!

Activity 1: write about a kettle using the characteristics you would choose to describe a particular family member, like your mother or grandfather.

Activity 2: write about a bicycle but describe it like you would describe a cat.

WRITING PROMPTS

Like figurative speech, writing prompts are another way to stimulate ideas and can enhance the writing process for any poet or writer. A writing prompt is an idea or sentence beginning that someone else has written and you have to finish that sentence off.

I used writing prompts quite a lot when I was starting out with my poetry. The poems I keep or consider final aren't the ones with writing prompts, but the prompts are what the ideas began with and they helped to get my creative thinking cap on.

Here's a list of prompts that I have created just for you. There are sentence starters and themes to get you underway with your poetry:

- The moon and the sea ...
- A flower that has only three days to live ...
- Falling off my bike was like ...

- Your first memory of the beach
- An imaginary event, like being the first person to travel to a faraway galaxy
- A cat who is best friends with a mouse
- Your dream car
- Your day at school
- An issue that's important to you, like environmentalism or humanitarianism
- A remix of your most-loved or most-hated childhood nursery rhyme
- While listening to a song, rewrite the lyrics to the tune/rhythm/beat
- Write from someone else's point of view, like your brother, sister, a famous person, or someone you admire

Writer's Block

So, let's talk about one of the hardest parts of writing—writer's block. It's a fairly common thing that happens to writers. Basically, it's not knowing where to start when writing, or sometimes ideas won't come to you because you're worrying too much about the end result.

I suffered from writer's block when I was writing new poems for the 2017 NSW Australian Poetry Slam state finals. I really wanted to capture the audience's attention and raise awareness of issues that are important to me, but I think I put too much pressure on myself. Not being able to write or make progress on something you're writing can come from self-made blockages, like too much pressure, a fear of failing, or just nerves.

You might've already experienced writer's block when doing things like staring at the computer screen for ages, or drawing silly things on the paper instead of progressing with the work you're trying to tackle.

When I get writer's block, it's like my brain has closed for the day: "no more bright ideas for sale, please come back tomorrow!" And once I had it for about a month. I spent hours writing, but nothing good came out of it. Just a heap of mess on paper. ☹

The good news is that the experience helped me to learn ways I can tackle writer's block. And writing prompts, like I've mentioned earlier in the chapter, are just the beginning to opening up your creative side.

My top 10 ways to help manage writer's block:

1. Write somewhere different
   Creative flow can come from different surroundings. Take your work to the beach, park, or a local cafe to break up your regular routine. Depending on what type of person you are, working in a quiet or busy location can help.

I love it when we go to the beach because I seem to write heaps of good stuff there. I also used to have a strange favorite place to write. A couple of years ago, I had a go-kart in my backyard and I would sit on it in the sun and just write—ideas always flowed when I was by myself.

2. Do something you love

It's a good idea to leave your writing and do something else you enjoy. Going for a bike ride, drawing, or cooking can relieve the stress caused by not knowing what to write about. And in doing something different, new inspirations might come to you.

3. Try to write a terrible poem

This writing exercise is the best! What you do is you try to see how badly you can write. Let yourself write badly by removing anything you think you "should" do and just write whatever comes to you. It can be easier to write knowing you are not going to put it into your poem. This will take the pressure off trying to make every sentence perfect. When I look back at one of my first poems now, I realize it wasn't one of my best pieces ... yeah, it was really terrible. Oh, you wanna hear it? Uh, okaaaay.

CITY
No trees are in sight
Cars and trucks rushing past me
Trafic lights beeping.

It even had a spelling error!

4. Set a deadline
   Think about when you want to have a poem finished. Some people work better under pressure so deadlines can push them to come up with ideas quickly. I like using fake deadlines. For example, if you need to submit a poem for your class project by next Friday, pretend that it's due a few days beforehand, like on Wednesday, that way you're giving yourself some extra days in case you need them. And a little pressure might get you motivated to write sooner.

5. Write in dot points
   I find that writing sentences, topics, ideas, or thoughts in dot points often helps me to create a structure for the poem in progress. It can be simpler to jot down your thoughts quickly as points instead of putting them straight into the poem. And they're easier to refer back to than reading through pages of messy notes.

6. **Write about the most boring thing ever**

Think of an everyday item, like a toaster or a light switch, and see if you can write about it and make it interesting. This can help with opening up the creative side of the brain.

7. **Get inspired**

Think about someone or something that inspires you and use that inspiration to write. I'm inspired by the news and the problems in our world that need our immediate help, like poverty or the destruction of innocent forests. And sometimes I just get inspiration from really random things.

The idea for my poem "Australian Air" started when I was doing some meditation and deep breathing (because I was stressing about my writing) and I just thought about what I knew about air and how vital it is for our bodies. That's when I thought of the line: *"we breathe in, we breathe out."*

8. **Eliminate distractions**

It's common to get distracted when you're trying to write. Your writing time is important, so treat it that way. Ask your parents to give you some quiet time—and watch their faces. I'm sure they've never heard that one from you before!

9. Just have fun

You may find you're too serious. This is my biggest hurdle, as sometimes I take my writing too seriously because I love it so much. Try to make writing enjoyable and add humor to your work. Make yourself laugh, and maybe the rest of the world too. ☺

10. Hang out with friends

When writer's block hits, hang out with your friends because it can shift energy, removing the unwanted blockages. When you come back to your writing, you'll hopefully have a fresh mind.

The more I practice these types of writing activities, the more comfortable I am with the creative writing process. So see what works for you and keep at it. Finding a comfortable space to write is important for your work because the right space will help you to relax, and then the creativity will flow. And speaking of relaxing, don't forget to remove distractions or try playing your favorite music while you write, because creating the ultimate writing space will be a long-term reward.

And remember that a lot of what comes to you creatively can be helped by you believing in yourself. I've found that I can usually handle writing pressures, but sometimes when that's combined with other commitments in my life, there's too much pressure overall. Finding the balance is really important, and when I started writing it took me about a year to work this out.

When I was in Year 6, I signed up for everything ... I was the school captain and debating team captain, I already played tennis competitively and travelled across the state most weekends in tennis season. I was also in a hip-hop dance group, the school choir, did weekly saxophone lessons, was in the school band, and I had two lead roles in my school plays.

(Breathe!)

Even though that year was one of the best years ever, I learned that I was under too much pressure all of the time. So now, I just have a healthy amount of pressure and also some down time too. It's all about balance, right?!

And, as always, breathing helps.

chapter 4
PERFORMING

Stage fright (noun)
Uncontrollable fear or nervousness before
performing for an audience.

Sometimes in slam poetry, the journey between your
first ideas and the end goal of performing can be
hard. One hurdle could be writer's block, which can
make you feel frustrated, irritated, and angry. You
find yourself staring at a frozen cursor or an empty
page and falling asleep to the clock ticking. It's no
fun when you have a boiling brain ready to implode.
And if you've gone through all that and managed
to craft an awesome poem you're about to perform,
then stage fright kicks in, well, that's a whole new
boiling temperature!

NERVES

Most people find it hard to read their poems out loud in front of their own family or friends, let alone to an audience of strangers. Nerves can come at any time for a performer—before or even during the event. Nerves like this can result in mumbling, freezing, sweating, and talking very quietly or too loudly and too fast. For me, nerves used to make me forget my lines or I'd get that squirmy feeling in my stomach. Once I forgot some lines halfway through a poem, but luckily I didn't panic. I just looked at the audience, breathing calmly and thinking about which line I was up to. I heard later that the audience thought I included that silent moment on purpose, which made the performance really exciting—a bonus!

Even though nerves are powerful and can interfere with your performance, there are many ways to help relieve and manage them beforehand and also on stage. When you first perform one of your poems, you may feel your heart skip a beat every second that goes by, or overthinking might even cause you to forget your lines. But if you can find a method of managing your nerves that works for you, you'll never look back. Perhaps someday I'll see you rip it up on stage!

One poet I know who has travelled the world

performing her poetry likes to dance backstage before she performs. And a couple of slam poets I've met wear headphones before they compete to block out sounds of the crowd or to distract themselves with their favorite music. There are many different ways to help combat public speaking nerves.

Here are some things I've tried before:

- Know your material: rehearse, rehearse, rehearse. Practice in front of a mirror or in front of family or friends
- Know who you'll be performing for, the size of the audience, and if media people, like journalists, will be there
- Know when you are expected on stage, and when to leave the stage
- Breathe in—breathe out

I believe that you can perform the same poem a thousand times, but the difference between the first time and the thousandth time is the way the performer handles nerves. A good performer will have a list of things they know helps them to overcome nerves and blockages. And remember, sometimes you'll just have a bad day—and that's okay too.

My top 10 ways to help manage nerves:

1. Be confident

   Try not to judge your work or worry about what others might think. Worrying can build up nerves more and more before the event. Being confident in your work will have a dramatic effect on your energy.

2. Take a look before performing

   Nerves sometimes come from a fear of the unknown, so research your audience and the location. Seeing where you're going to perform might relieve nerves.

3. Rehearse

   Practice in front of a mirror, in the car, on the bus, when you wake up, when you brush your teeth—find every opportunity you can to rehearse your performance.

4. Have fun

   Once you've rehearsed enough, it's a good idea to take your mind off things and do something you love on the day that you'll be performing. Listening to music or taking a walk can help distract the mind. This will build your confidence because it will create trust in your own ability.

5. **Make sure you're not thirsty or hungry**

   Try to keep hydrated and eat something leading up to your performance. Nerves may make you feel dizzy or sick if you don't have food in your tummy. Sipping small amounts of water will allow you to perform without having a dry mouth and dry lips. I've found dryness can stop you from being able to speak easily on stage, which can interrupt your flow.

6. **Keep moving**

   Jogging on the spot, walking around, or jumping up and down can help remove nerves or anxiety. I danced backstage before the 2017 National Australian Poetry Slam. The MC, Arielle Cottingham, shared a massive amount of performance experience with us and she suggested we move about. This helped me to learn how to calm my nerves in a brand-new way.

7. **Don't overthink**

   If you're backstage and waiting to perform, try not to go over your lines. If you go over them too often, it may cause you to forget them (weird, I know!) and then you'll be even more anxious to step onto the stage.

8. Practice mindfulness

Mindfulness can be practiced anywhere and at any time. Slow down your thoughts and focus on your breathing. Think about experiencing the moment and nothing else. It can help to close your eyes and take long deep breaths, blocking out surrounding sounds and thinking of calming things, like waves or the ocean. (Unless you have a fear of the water ... then think of something else!)

9. Take your time

When on stage, I deliberately pause before starting my performance. I take three deep breaths and focus my eyes on my toes, which helps me to feel centered and gets my brain ready. Never feel pressured to start the moment you walk onstage, as the audience will happily wait.

10. Use hand movements

Using your hands to express certain sentences or words can help to release nerves. It can also show emotion in your story and make your overall performance more appealing.

11. BONUS TIP—Find what works for you

Everyone is different, which means everyone will have different types of nerves. Try out some of these tips and see what works.

EMOTION

Feeling nervous is an emotion that performers try to avoid, and one way to move away from nerves is to focus on other emotions that you want your audience to feel when they hear your poem. Projecting the right emotions could be the difference between a good slam poem and a winning slam poem. A strong use of emotion through facial expressions, hand movements, and tone of voice can help to make the audience feel all the feels—happy, sad, excited, angry, inspired, depressed, or uplifted.

Gaining the audience's interest in the poem is also just as important as having the opportunity to perform your poetry. In my poems, I use fast stanzas or paragraphs at certain points. Changing up the tone and using different speeds when reciting a poem can leave the audience eagerly waiting for the next word. I don't really know how I came up with the idea of speaking quickly when I first started rhyming and writing slam poetry, but I liked how it made my poems more interesting than if they had just the same slow cadence throughout.

Remember, some words or topics might have indicator emotions where you can add specific movements as you speak to enhance the interpretation. Try not to overdo it though, as it's about finding a balance between speaking your poem and expressing it. And this takes practice. An easy way to get good at this is to record your poem (use that phone you've always got in your hand!) and play it back to hear how it's sounding.

Also think about how you stand on stage. A good performer will make eye contact with the audience, have strong facial expressions that support the tone of the story, use body gestures, and, as previously mentioned, change up the rhythm of the poem so it's not all at one pace—just like how a song has different tempos throughout.

Some poets also include rhetorical questions and audience participation parts in their performances. This can strengthen the bond between audience and performer. I like to include pauses or moments of silence in certain poems to allow the audience time to reflect on what's being said. It gives people space to think and can add a sense of drama too.

When I performed at the Adelaide Fringe Festival, I was lucky enough to work with the tremendously talented multi-instrumentalist Adam Page, who mixed music with one of my poems. As a musician myself, I was so excited when I visited Adam's studio and he had literally every instrument you could think of! We chose to use a looping machine as well as some other instruments, and when we performed together we had the best time ever! We freestyled, which meant we actually made it all up on the spot. Adam calls it improvisation, which was really liberating for me as I spend a lot of time perfecting my poems and my performances. But I often imagine my poems turning into songs, so I was also comfortable with this creative angle.

Having the ability to ignite your emotions and put them into words and actions is like a car with fuel ... it will take you places! And there are so many ways to work on performing your poetry that you'll always be learning new things when you perform in front of different audiences and at a variety of venues. One of the best things you will notice at any slam is that everyone is different, so be confident in what you can bring and own it!

chapter 5
OPPORTUNITY

Opportunity (noun)

The moment a new and exciting experience is offered.

There's something special about walking onto a stage. Mixed emotions and jumbled thoughts float around your head as you take a look at the audience. Then clarity hits and sharing your poem is all that you can do ... all you want to do.

In the introduction of this book, I spoke about my amazing experience performing at the Sydney Opera House. Well, since then things have just exploded for me and I've been able to learn so much from each writing and performing experience. I'm lucky to have the opportunity to talk about the issues that concern me by sharing my poems on TV, at festivals, and at other events, such as TEDxSydney 2018. One aspect that I've been really surprised by is everyone's positive response. I had so much fun filming a TV interview for "Behind the News" and they also posted the segment on social media, which was viewed in schools and online over 135,000 times in the first week. That blows my mind right out of the Southern Hemisphere!

I've also had the chance to learn some amazing things and challenge myself, like when I memorized four poems to perform at a festival—usually I'd only perform one or two at a time. Pushing my memory to the test, I felt comfortable on the day once I knew that I could recite all four even if there were lots of distractions. My mum has this funny way of testing if I'm ready to perform. I rehearse and she tries her hardest to distract me. When I don't pause or flinch, I'm ready. As a performer I prefer no disruptions when I write and perform, but life doesn't always give you what you want. I had a really solid writing flow this morning, for example, then my mum started making one of her healthy smoothies. The moment the sound of the blender hit my eardrums, I lost where I was up to with my thoughts and my flow basically became as smooshed as the ingredients in the smoothie!

When I think back on all of my performances,

the biggest audience I've ever been in front of was at the XXI Commonwealth Games Closing Ceremony on the Gold Coast. That event was epic! The stadium audience was 35,000 people and the performance was also televised live to 1.5 billion people worldwide. Over the past couple of years I've learned to deal with nerves, but they were certainly pretty mega during this performance.

Between me and you, I think nerves are a way of letting us know that something important is about to happen, and it's just our bodies reminding us that we care about that important thing, whatever it might be. In learning how to manage nerves and distractions, I've been fortunate enough to get the opportunity to share my thoughts about the world on a public platform.

Because I'm passionate about raising awareness for equality, deforestation, climate change, and the war on waste, I've chosen to take a positive stance for change. I believe we all need to make a stand in the areas important to our everyday lives. Basically, *how* we choose to handle these topics is going to have the biggest impact on our future.

You don't have to donate a million dollars to charity or become prime minister to help create a nationwide policy restricting single-use plastic bags—although giving to charities and becoming a political leader are pretty cool too! There are so many ways to look after our planet and the environment that every person can be a part of.

In my household, we try to buy fruit and vegetables that are not in plastic wrapping and food that hasn't got too much packaging. We've eliminated the use of cling wrap and other plastic products, and when we buy takeaway drinks from our local cafe, we bring our own cups from home to use.

Another way I try to help create a positive impact on our planet is by picking up trash. Some people might laugh at this or think it's icky, but when we walk my dog, Mum and I carry a reusable bag to collect any litter or plastic that we see. We have a little saying for when we pick up gross stuff—"better our hands dirty than our planet." These are the little things that if enough of us do today, will have the biggest ever impact on tomorrow.

Trying to find a way that you can help is the best thing *you* can do. Apart from doing small everyday things, I try to help raise awareness of important topics by writing about them in my poetry. I hope my work might plant thought-seeds in people's heads that may not have been there before. These new ideas could potentially grow and encourage them to do something about the issues they're concerned with. And maybe they'll become a game changer too.

The opportunity for each of us to create change

is present in our daily choices. Something that we've seen throughout every important movement of history is that people power has a huge effect, so I encourage everyone to get involved and create change to make tomorrow better than today.

After so many opportunities and experiences, my motivation and passion for writing to raise awareness of topics I believe in has continued to grow. And my love for poetry is growing just as much, even though I know there's a lot more to learn. All of these opportunities have proven to me that dreams can come true, so yours can too! Be a game changer with me and make tomorrow better than today by putting your ideas, thoughts, and beliefs into the limelight.

Here's the poem I wrote for my biggest opportunity to date for reaching people with my poetry, the closing ceremony of the 2018 Commonwealth Games:

To Unite, Like Uniting Is A Sport

Sshh—sshh—sshh
The waves turned to gold, as the sun rose, across the land.

But not just any land,
Land—where you can find sea mist, city vibes, and rainforest haze
in one place.
Land of history that goes back far, with a future where we all reach for the stars, in
our Southern Cross.
Land where you can find multiculturalism in a team
without   a   single   limitation.
Land of People Power, always empowering a powerful change around our great
mountain ranges and across.

Hhhh … Hhhhh … Hhhhh …

And then I heard something.

Brrrrbrrrrbrbrbrrrrbrbrrr …

The earthquake shakes, thunder awakes, that makes, fast-flowing ripples in the lakes.
This was a time, when I got shivers down my spine, as I watched these hard-working athletes shine, and celebrated the Commonwealth nations who brought together sporting that was – divine.

I stand proudly here with you.
In sharing their dreams, because
this is where they came alive …
This is where athletes came together and together they
strived …
They strived because their passion has inspired them,
since the day they arrived, and by carrying this
inspiration, they've spread
motivation – helping change thousands of lives.

But   that's just the beginning …

When you realize happiness is GIVING, and sport is
your life's underpinning, and add that onto your innings,
you'll be springing, swinging, and singing, as you spend
your whole life grinning, watching gymnasts spinning,
swimmers swimming, making a splash! Electricity sparks
as sprinters dash, when they finish in a flash.

And just feeling the energy makes you excited.
Everyone's delighted,

because here on the Gold Coast,
we stand
together—united.

To unite, like uniting is a sport.
Because with uniting instead of dividing, this is where we come, when we work not
together, but to work together as **one.**
Taking a moment from greed, you can realize how far you've come.
And your life as a person, **has only just begun.**

I'm here because of *you*, I'm here because of *me*, but *together* we are **greater** than
what we could ever individually be.
Let us rise out of our seats and chase our dreams because they're here to be
chased no matter how hard it seems.

It's now time to say goodbye, to the trees, the seas, and the Gold Coast sky.
As we leave to achieve our dreams through the rest of our lives. Carrying these memories that will never fade.

Because this was real passion.
This was unforgettable champions.
This was true sportsmanship.

This was our story, being made.

POEMS BY ME, SOLLI RAPHAEL

Most of my poems come from days, weeks, and months of jotting down ideas, quotes, dot points, and sentences whenever they randomly come to my mind. All of these poems have been created and written throughout 2017 and 2018, capturing my emotions, experiences, and beliefs.

Note about format of poems:
the *italics* indicate the sections to be sung and the condensed lines show fast-tempo sections.

WELCOME TO THE WONDERFUL WORLD OF POETRY

Welcome to the wonderful world of poetry!
Welcome to the wonderful world of poetry!
Welcome to the wonderful world of poetry!
Welcome to the wonderful world of poetry!

They call it the language of rhythm; words of meaning,
thoughts and sound symbolism.
Throughout history, power has occurred through words
where from the depths poets have risen.
Overcoming crusades and problems, though this is no
algorithm.
This is greatness.
This is verses and stanzas.
This is artists using words to seize an empty canvas.
For those who have changed circumstances,
for those who've been abandoned,
for those who are going through cancer,
for those who wanted chances and for those who have
a passion to make a change and want to change their
actions.

This is for you.
A place where everyone belongs.
A language to live and pursue. Give and renew.

A world of equality.
And a future of greatness for all of us to continue.

Welcome to the wonderful world of poetry!
Welcome to the wonderful world of poetry!
Welcome to the wonderful world of poetry!
Welcome to the wonderful world of poetry!

They call it pen and paper. A busy cursor. A literature
educator.
An odyssey, further prophecies for equality,
like philosophies.

Poetry economies grow to possibly help ecology
globally, and rhyming archaeology grows to differ
politics. Political policies can be described as comedy
to those who create a colony to serve it with prosody
ferocity which can make harmony grow with generosity
to fight dishonesty,
fighting for those who live in proper poverty, fighting for
those with no proper property, fighting for those who
think that we obviously need to save our world properly.
Because this is poetry.

Welcome to the wonderful world of poetry!
Welcome to the wonderful world of poetry!
Welcome to the wonderful world of poetry!

Welcome to the wonderful world of poetry!

Through stresses and rhymes there's a power to find,
hiding between the rhyme schemes and lines.
From your mind to the readers' eyes, let a message appear.
Because these are words of experiences, passions, and ideas.
To help the world rise above and shine.

Because this is creative writing.
Writing where you can create something exciting.
From the moment you start writing or typing
to the moment you're reciting to the moment when
you're sighting the audience while alighting and igniting
a spark to embark on a journey that's delighting.

This is poetry.

Welcome to the wonderful world of poetry!
Welcome to the wonderful world of poetry!
Welcome to the wonderful world of poetry!
Welcome to the wonderful world of poetry!

LIMELIGHT

That feeling of walking out onto a stage.
Echoing footsteps with bright lights shining down
on you like the sun's rays in an empty field.
The audience waiting for your first word, first
movement, first rhythm.

In the limelight.

Whether it's a stage small enough to be able to step up
onto with one small step.
Whether it's a stage just on the plain floor, with your
friends and family watching you with just a fraction of a
smile.
Whether it's a stage so big that it feels like you walked
to the moon and back before you reach the microphone
stand.
A stage so big that thousands among millions among
billions of people are watching your every move,
every feeling, every step.
A stage so famous that the whole world knows about it,
wants to see it, wants to experience its glory.
A stage you imagine being on and every move you take
the audience cheers louder and louder, when you're
having a good dream in a deep sleep.

A stage with such a large audience, you feel like a fly you can just hear, buzzing in the kitchen. And just thinking about it gives you shivers down your spine.

That stage you've been waiting your whole life to be standing on.

Every word you speak, every action you make, you take a step forward with your feet, just a little closer to the limelight.

Are you going to use this limelight as your authority?
To change the rules. To end poverty.
'cause honestly,
this controversy is making the majority—priority.

But if we take jealousy out of our legacy we might just find **equality**.
And empower your power. Let it be sweet not sour.
Make it your superpower and let positivity rule every minute of every hour.
Stop and smell the roses, stop and smell the flowers, because life's not a rush, life has greatness to encounter.

Are you going to be a gamechanger?
Are you going to be a gamechanger?

Be a gamechanger?
Gamechanger?
Use this limelight!
Use this limelight!
Use this limelight!
Use this limelight!
Limelight!

Are you ready to go?
Ready to go and show the world that there's an opinion
to help change grow.
Why?
Because there's a goal higher than the night sky.
And to supply, apply or rely on information from
something that doesn't even have eyes.
We need to see that there's more than lies and spies and
cutting trees.
And yet we're still struggling to try and be someone we
don't even know.
And let your passions be your actions that leave you and
the world with matching satisfaction.

Are you going to be a gamechanger?
Are you going to be a gamechanger?
Be a gamechanger?
Gamechanger?
Use this limelight!
Use this limelight!

Use this limelight!
Use this limelight!
Limelight!

The future needs you and me, to create equality
across all levels of humanity.
Take some audacity to stick into your reality, and to
stay sane we sometimes need,
change.
Because to resolve the unsolved it involves and revolves
around evolution.
And by making a contribution, you're planting a seed,
placing a thought in people's brains that was not there
before.
Seize this moment, live it and own it, and if you leave the
"um" till the end of the moment, you might just create
enough momentum.
To take flight to great heights on a stage to speak your
truth in the limelight.

Are you going to be a gamechanger?
Are you going to be a gamechanger?
Be a gamechanger?
Gamechanger?
Use this limelight!
Use this limelight!
Use this limelight!
Use this limelight!
Limelight!

EVOLUTION

BANG!
    That's the sound of evolution, it shouldn't lead to
confusion, but thanks to your contribution—we've
found a solution for the word *evolution*.

Now to get evolution,
you need to do something that's unique and new,
like inventing a psychotic robotic barbecue,
or an antibiotic azotic beef stew to get rid of the flu and
make you feel fresh and new.

Since the day we arrived,
we've been finding ways to survive …
        and we've strived to stay alive with water and fire,
things that we can hire,
washers and dryers, motors and tires, sellers and buyers
and people who we admire.

We seem to have a desire of being above the high wire,
though some are relaxing and others are faxing taxes
even though
the price is getting higher and higher.
But humans
humans are still willing to believe we can achieve much
more than we can perceive to conceive.

Some people can weave,
some people can play a semibreve,
while others wear short sleeves on a sick leave,
Monday-itis … I believe.

We've been through wars and storms,
and have opened doors, to your new house
with two floors
that you bought for more than you could afford
        —turns out the house is in a bad position,
has a horrible mold condition and is going under
demolition.
Maybe the agent faked their acquisition.
     Oh dear, wasn't that a bad decision?
          Should of listened to your intuition.

Some decisions in life
     get us into strife,
          but that's what makes us
smarter
     and more able,
          to enable
the links between the future and the fable on a table,
instead of in the jungle that's unstable
                    and unable to get internet access
                              through a
                                   cable.

Throughout history, we've succeeded and we've failed,
and you're just finding that out on Wikipedia, in great detail,
while you choke on the air that you've just inhaled.
Because of the air pollution—

it's a BIG prosecution,

but we've found elocutions
just to tell the world we're finding a solution
for pollution
on our convolution
as a counter-revolution and retribution.

All for one thing …
TO PROVE EVOLUTION.

GAME CHANGER

I am a gamechanger.
I am a game change, change game, low age, no rage,
onstage arranger.
I am both yes and no, stay and go, catch and throw,
goodbye and hello, forest ranger.
I am the lightning that makes thunder—rumble.
I am the space—outside of the box.
I am the magnetic field between the moon and the sea.
I am the quality—in equality.
I am the undiscovered myth in wordsmith.
I am the reality, of my own big dreams.
I am the curve of the world, that I can only just see.
I am a gamechanger.
I am a curly hair very rare level of sublimity.
I am a square of fresh air.
I am the fair in share, a spare pair of prayers for stairs to
infinity.
I am a gamechanger.
And no matter how much **you** change,
No matter how much the **world** changes,
No matter how much **change** changes.
I will always be changing, as, **I**, am a gamechanger.

Australian Air

Air
    it's the invisible goodness, that links our brain
with full gain,
so we can think without a strain,
and without it, we would probably go insane.

And it goes through our blood veins,
and acts like a water main,
the more we get, the more our plants grow,
the more our cells grow,
the more **we** grow,
in wealth and health,

and although our lives are stressful and pressurized with
anxiety and control, and you're still working on relaxing
your soul, while running around the magnetic pole,
looking for your self-control, and although it's taking its toll,
we still breathe.

We breathe in, we breathe out

Since the day of our arrival, we've been killing our own
survival, and it's vital, that our sidle title is put aside, so
we can become ONE with our rivals.

We breathe in, we breathe out

So don't sit around waiting for your life to caper, instead—
grab your pens and your paper—your voices and your eyes,
so we can reach for the sky, and look down on the world,
and tell them why,
we need to make a change

      to our lives.

Because we don't have to be these average everyday
humans anymore

we can show this world what we feel, see, and think,

and that might be the hidden link,
between peace, war, and humans causing our own race to
be extinct.

And sometimes
    we need to breathe out,
        just so we can breathe in kindness
and passion.

Because this Australian air is polluted with,
                    choking from our own depression,
and if we don't fight for our rights ... it's like mixing
hemimorphite and pegmatite, so that you can think as
fast as the speed of light, but if you're not speaking your
own sight, even though you might despite the fright to
be polite and rewrite how we should reunite, we may as
well do a plebiscite, for if we should keep celebrating

how the blacks were killed by the whites.

So—
get out of your seats,
rise up,
open your windows,
let fresh air flood your homes, flood your lungs,
flood your brains!

Change the way you think,
CHANGE the way you LIVE.
Open your eyes and breathe out yesterday's air,
and—breathe in—Today's
Opportunities.

TREE TRUNKS' TRUST: PART ONE

Trees are true.
Tree trunks are true.
Tree Trunks' Trust is tricky, but true.
Tree Trunks' Trust is so trustworthy, that it's stronger
than superglue.
The tree trunks try to keep their trust trustworthy,
but trying isn't new.
With all these modern troubles, Tree Trunks' Trust
is troubled too.

The tree trunks try and try, but their—trust just isn't
trustworthy, and their tracks aren't trustworthy either,
with all these tractors and chain saws following their
tracks, a new trust is due.

The tree trunk population is tripling, but the human
population is tripling too.
And the demand of tree trunk products, is troubling the
Tree Trunks' Trust.
What we humans don't realize, is when Tree Trunks'
Trust dies, we die too.
And a troubling tragedy will occur, if we don't replace
paper and wood glue.
The Tree Trunks' Trust team has decided.
They are all leaving, to embark on a journey that's
unknown.

The Tree Trunks' Trust team depart, to take back their forest thrown.

To make humans realize that trees are worth more than the timber price shown.

Though trillions of trees have died, trillions more try to make it through.

But to make it any further

The Trees Need You.

Maybe

Our expectations are based on the things we have.

Our gratitude seems to only be determined on whether we're happy or sad.

Only our experiences tell whether things are good or bad.

But whether ...

The weather is better now or never, since ever, forever, whenever and wherever we should altogether endeavor to use our treasure to better our errors however, you can't measure how clever you are. Be centered as we enter a new stage in society.

Without contrariety.
Finally, we move silently and quietly through the darkness of the day.

And maybe one day,
we will find a way to pray to the name, and display our

way to better our fate.

Yet straightaway we inveigh whatever we hate, so much that we untie a lace and separate the world just a little more day by day.

But if we try and say our truths in a way that conveys a spray of okays then the future might be better than today.

So, if tomorrow was a giveaway, you would know that today would be the same.

Maybe.

Through the Sea, Was a City

Through the sea, was a city, through the city, there was he.
Through he, there was the public, through the public,
there was poverty.
Through poverty, there was money, through money,
there was greed,
Through greed, there were problems, through problems,
there was a need.
Through that need, there was poverty, through poverty,
there was money and a negative circular economy.
Through that negative circular economy, there were
crusades, through crusades, there were tragedies,
through tragedies, there were keys.
Through the keys, there was a future, through the future,
there was a plea,
Through that plea, there was a city—a city wanting
change and change is what they need.
Through that need, there was the public, through the
public, there was a change,
Through that change, there was people power.
Through people power, there was a key,
Through that key, there was the future, through that
future, there was a city:
A city of people power, and through that city, there was
the sea.

Embrace Our Differences

It was a nice sunny day, as I felt the gentle touch of the sand,
as I sat there peacefully, without a phone in my hand.
A day felt like an hour, and a swim felt so exquisite, and it
was like time wasn't even existent.

When do you relax, and have a   decent   rest?
When do you take a break, and get that pressure off your chest?

Because it seems to me, we've only progressed in stress,
and all our ideas are currently being compressed, in big
factories that have chemically enhanced genes, with
giant machines,
and
our government should take the blame,
for making us all the same, even though we don't want to
be like the rest.

So, with no further claim, we should all be ashamed,
because you could ask a nurse, doctor, or scientist,
and they'll all tell you, no two brains are the same.

There's our future sitting at school, programmed to
worry about tests, our past still waiting for an apology for
being distressed, the homeless still feeling dispossessed,
the refugees who aren't impressed, as the government

can't even make them feel blessed.

The everyday heroes: who don't get heard when their
ideas are expressed, and people who suggest that we
behest—the—best.

Because we need to embrace our differences and make
our differences count,
and although we're not a paramount,
and the world and love aren't a tantamount.

We need to make our surmounts our fount
of inspiration and affirmation, because it's up to you to
turn a pen into a donation, and make every last dollar
count.

Don't justify your quantity of quality frivolities, because
inequality and equality policies' polity isn't jollity or
prodigality, and a colony's odyssey of psychological
honesty is honestly an oddity.

So, when you've finished fighting for your rights and
differentiating your differences.
Transform your pens, let history help our future, speak
to those who don't want to listen,

And   Embrace   Our   Differences.

Go!

The speaker shouts and as we all know,
our determination is about to put on a show,
as our legs run with speed and flow,
but first I throw myself forward, with a moderate pace.
I embrace the air and chase my pacer and first place of
the race.

My shoelace is tied, I'm focus-eyed and decide to take
the inside lane.
I'm able to obtain my form, without a strain and my
temperature is only warm,
I could have sworn this was a miracle, but it's not satirical,
it's months of training, early mornings of maintaining
speed,
whether it's sunny or raining, without complaining
I chose to proceed.

I pass the 5.5-kilometer mark, as I take a stop for a sugar
drink, I start to think about my training plan,
and lacked a breath, but still, I ran.

I pass the 8-kilometer mark and pick up speed as I enter
the home run.
The real competition begun, I overtook runners, one by

one.
My legs felt like they weighed a ton, but I continued in
the boiling sun
sprinting toward the final stretch of the run.

9.5-kilometers.
The finish line is in sight.
It took a while but had to still fight.

Media Literacy: Fake News

We are in a day and age where lots of time is spent on devices, and as the rate of fake news rises, to evolve, we must get involved, in finding ways to determine safe sites online.
Thoughts bloom, as kids and teens gather in classrooms, on a journey for news young Australians can consume.

Times change, as we all arrange, an action plan to open a new page, for the government.

Soon Australia will discover it, more news without scary scenes and harsh judgment.

And fake news is so hard to spot, hardly anyone can uncover it.

Lots of organizations.

Help us to be an up-to-date nation, with kid-friendly information, to provide inspiration and motivation for this generation.

As this is an important realization, before it's too late.

We're saving the date, by putting ideas on our plates, and plans to create, a way without the wait, to save our fate, with the rate of click bait, a debate that relates awaits and navigates its way to the government's gates.

And with all this white noise, we're starting to lose our voice, but if we gather all the girls and boys and make the right choice, we will all be up to date, and that's a time to rejoice.

So, are you going to wait for that day?

Are you going to turn your head and play?
Watch the news, which is only just okay, are you going to make it that way, wait for the times to pay, are you going to meet us halfway?

Seize each day, change the game.

Because no matter how many days you live, not one will be the same.

We Can Be More!

We can be more.
We can be more than nice packaging on our wasted
products.
We can be more than paper cuts and paper cups.
We can be more than a "more pollution" solution.
We can be more than plastic bags, tagging flags all over
our sea life population.

We can be more than an idea about a waste diminution,
discussing a future revolution and a future resolution,
confusion because evolution is just a proven allusion
about how our home will soon be ruins.

But we can be more.

We can be more than trying to ignore the war on waste.
We can be more than a future of haste, moving us
toward a disaster being complete.
And we throw out a third of the food we eat.
That is more disgusting than the sweat amongst our feet.

It's true—
YOU think it's up to the factories
but it's really   up   to   **you.**

So next time you go into the shops,
think about all the crops, ripped-off farmers, plastic bags,
and those who dedicate their lives to the war on waste
they pursue.

Because it's all in **People Power.** People have the power
to make the people greedy or equals, through the sequels
of our days, changing our ways, can rephrase our answer,
to yes.
Yes, I will change, opening a new page, starting a new
stage, entering a new age, in saving our **world**.
Because this is something we can't erase, and yet we're
still choosing money over something that's irreplaceable,
and here it looks all right, but over there it's disgraceful.

Because our home is dying.
Our ice caps are crying. Our ecosystems are sighing,
while we keep buying,
keeping our business ships sailing, but our tips are failing
to maintain our rubbish.
When did our planet deserve to be punished?
Yet they say everything's "fine."

Don't listen to our planet, we will never need to change,
we will never need to change because everything will
always stay the same.
And then it's gone.

But we can still be more!

We can be more than throwing our mistakes on the dockside.
We can be more than travelling through carbon dioxide with carbon monoxide.
We can be more than bypassing the fact that global warming is a global warning of heat.
And if you can't conceive it, doesn't mean you shouldn't believe it. Because we can change coal mines to solar inclines by taking a step with our feet.
We can be more because our home is infinity to what money could ever be worth.
And realize that your litter is a bitter pinch to the earth.

We can be more than this.

We can be more.

Can't we?

Tree Trunks' Trust: Part Two

The Tree Trunks' Trust team take some time to talk.

To take two minutes to think about the direction that
they should walk.

The track ahead is tough; an untamed thick terrain.
Covered in traffic lights, tree choppers, and those who
are inhumane.

They thought their roots were moving them toward
their destination, but then their GPS shouted, "root
recalculation!"

Off they went, in the right direction to form a projection
to bring attention to mention this complexion in the lack
of protection in the nearby selected section, they were
close.
They could feel it in their bark, from the day they
embarked from their roots to their sticks, they knew they
had to stick together.
It was the only way to make the situation better.
Oh!
They had made it!

The tree chopper factory was in sight.

Though it wasn't time to celebrate, it was time to fight for trees' rights!

They tried to get in, but the tree choppers' security told them to turn around and leave.

The Tree Trunks' Trust team's tree translator tried to tell them that this was important, but the security still did not believe.

But they weren't just going to give up, they were the Tree Trunks' Trust team with trust so trustworthy, that it's stronger than superglue.

They knew, that they were going to stand their ground and wait for the terrible tree tragedy to end and for an eco-friendly solution to be found.

They blocked the tree choppers' trucks and chain saws and tractors.

A protest had begun but the impact was
just not enough.

They tried to find a way to make it all stop.
But the factory had too much power, their plan had
become a flop.

There must be a solution.
Otherwise the world will become animal museums and a
big ball of pollution.

This was it, this was as much as they could do.
They had walked for days and hours, finding ways to
become empowered, but it was now up to the people to
match the tree choppers' factory with people power.

NEW RIPPLES

The earthquake shakes, the thunder awakes that makes,
fast-flowing ripples in the lakes.
It's a time where snakes take a break to awake, partake
and take no time to undertake change, knowing all's at
stake. With fake remakes and retakes to our non-opaque
mistakes.
But if only fear was on the line, we would all be fine.
'Cause it's a time where mine no longer shines and where
we redefine divine.
And whining declines when benign inclines.
Assign and align yourself, climb high and rise above,
'cause it's a one-time sublime prime time to define the
bottom line.
But until then, take a ride on these new ripples.

It's a rippling affect, a tripling effect, it deflects, reflects,
and directs some respect to everyone, and to those who
suspect none.
Protect what will be done.
Expect that we've begun.
It's a complex pun, connect fun, expect none, detect one,
a perfect sun.
This context stuns, with intellectual love.
So, rise above.

But until then, take a ride on these new ripples.
Please proceed.
Exceed and succeed.
Feed off the need, to spread seeds of good deeds.
Indeed, it's agreed, freed, and guaranteed.
Don't mislead or misread, just read between the lines,
but read out of them at the same time.

There's no crime to rhymes, so rhyme like it's your
only battle cry, like it's the meaning of a life that's simple.

But until then, take a ride on these new ripples
But until then, take a ride on these new ripples
But until then, take a ride on these new ripples
But until then, take a ride on these new ripples

CHANGES

Are we changing?
Are these changes, turning pages, for education, of all ages.
Without doubt.

Are we changing?
Are these changes, in new stages, going places, for all races.
Without doubt.

Because this is our future we're talking about.
Bullying solutions should have been found.
And it needs to be fixed, because this sort of thing just shouldn't
be allowed.
Are we changing?

Because to me we need to make a difference right now.

At first school sounded great, when we left to go.
But at the gates, we signed away our fate to someone we
didn't even know.
And there they were.
They called them bullies. Bulls filled with lies trying to
own you, with horns connected to their minds.
Piercing you with the devil in their eyes.

Which for them, it must have been fun. Watching kids
amongst the fingertips try,
to run
but couldn't.

And class was a simile for a legitimate, predicament,
imprisonment.
Stuck between bars of lessons where all you could do
was, sigh.

Though no one would notice me down, down so deep
I'm technically underground.
Buried under tidal waves of books and hurricanes of
tests. Massive floods of words, feeling every painful drip,
push me down, down into the puddles and down through
all the drains and out into the sea, struggling in the rips.

Too weak to make it through, too far to call out, you can
put your hand up, but the teacher might not ever answer.
Maybe teachers are just a feature for the school, or an
educational enhancer.
And the whole world finds out that there's a problem
before the teacher does.
It's like they're not even there, a hologram that breathes
air or a robot that has hair.

Or maybe it's me.

Because it's starting to feel like I'm in a different world,
hurled in and out of a porthole.
Like my pain is an invisible potion.
I had a commotion notion in my handwoven corrosion,
like a frozen motioned lotion ocean, with a devotion of a
chosen promotion token, and this was my only chance to
make an invisible potion explosion.

I got up and stood my ground but found that the
solution was abusion.

If I was given five dollars for every time I was bullied and
ten dollars for every time I was laughed at, I would be a
millionaire.

It's like I'm a hit from   a sitcom.
But I wasn't going to quit and run.
I felt like a   split gun. Made with the great power yet
damaged enough to be finished   and   done.
An anger kingdom. All I have to do is look at their throat,
and I could   slit   one.
And to think this is what school has become.
It's not fun.

Are we changing?
Are these changes, turning pages, for education, of all ages.

Without doubt.
Are we changing?
Are these changes, in new stages, going places, for all races.
Without doubt.

Because this is our future we're talking about.
Bullying solutions should have been found.
And it needs to be fixed, because this sort of thing just shouldn't
be allowed.

Are we changing?

Because to me we need to make a difference right now.

The floods have finished, and the fires have burned out.
Suicide rates climb higher and higher
and this is something we should all be worried about.

And to think all of this is normal. This is what you
should expect.
Being a victim of crime, and time can only tell when
you'll be hurt next.

Things need to change. Because change is the only one
calling out your name when all of your thoughts are

doubts.

Change is the only thing saving us from extinction. And if we work together we will forever be able to change our education, because our teaching is historic and if we take a glance at our future, you will find that right now we need to make a difference.

Are we changing?
Are these changes, turning pages, for education, of all ages.
Without doubt.

Are we changing?
Are these changes, in new stages, going places, for all races.
Without doubt.

Because this is our future we're talking about.
Bullying solutions should have been found.
And it needs to be fixed, because this sort of thing just shouldn't be allowed.

Are we changing?

Because to me we need to make a difference right now.

Are we changing?
Are these changes, turning pages, for education, of all ages.
Without doubt.

Are we changing?
Are these changes, in new stages, going places, for all races.
Without doubt.

Because this is our future we're talking about.
Bullying solutions should have been found.
And it needs to be fixed, because this sort of thing just shouldn't
be allowed.

Are we changing?

Because to me we need to make a difference right now.

Changes.

FLY.

Fly, they told me. Spread your wings, take off and.
Fly, go further, reach for the sun and be calm
enough to breathe enough air to, drift like a feather and.
Fly, let the wings of your mind and the feathers of your
soul make you.
Fly, lift off with your feet, look down with your eyes.
Enhance your freedom, let go, glide and.
Fly, breathe in the air that surrounds you, relax and
enjoy. Let the palms of your hands fly you through life
and.
Fly, gravitate toward your dreams and let air pockets
take you high enough to see the endless opportunities.
Grabbing hold of every speck of thrust to reach for your
star, looking down on your past, looking up toward your
future and.
Fly.
Let your feet boost you with the power within. Let your
words be fulfilled with belief, strong enough to clear
your path ahead.
And so high you now know that home isn't just four
walls with a bed and roof, but the place where your
dreams take you.

Now high enough to see that freedom is determined by not the fence around but the fence within.
Now high enough to have enough inspiration and determination to have them like feathers tight in your hand, growing more and more every day, that it's enough to make you.
Fly, they told me.
Fly.

ÁRBOL DE HELADO

Si helado creció en un árbol de helado, un árbol de
helado sería para mí.
Esto significa que puedo comer helado cuando quiera.

Que podía comer cada segundo, que no es un podría que
es un sí.

Tengo chocolate y menta, fresa y vainilla. Tendría cada
sabor, en mi selva de árboles helados.

Así que, si te gusta el helado, debe comprar un árbol
de helado. Tiene un sabor cremoso, que es realmente
bonito.

Porque si un árbol de helado es para mí, un árbol helado
es para ti, y si es un árbol de helado para ti, entonces un
árbol de helado es para mí.

GOODNIGHT

Calm your busy mind,
Because tomorrow awaits,
With only greatness.

WHEN THE SKY CAME ALIVE

The fifth season will soon arrive
When all four seasons meet.
It is then when the sky comes alive
And diverse weathers greet.

Down come the heavy rains
As the flowers start to bloom.
The sun shines on the windowpane
And the strong icy winds loom.

All different weather in one day,
Never knowing what to wear.
The sky changing from blue to gray
With strange temperatures in the air.
Together the weather comes to unite.
Together bringing new climates to excite.

A Split Second

Although it was only a flash, you soon start to wonder.
Why it felt like a year had passed, with sunshine, rain, and
thunder.

On the Rainbow

On the rainbow you will find

The untold secrets of the land
The power in your idea's hand
The serenity of a place unmanned
And what the future holds, no one knows.

The colored area where happiness flows
The studied arc where change grows
The showing of the final prose
And magic that will spark a delight.

The refreshing rain in sight
The sun's rays of warm light
The view from the great height
And breeze will leave you satisfied.

The stillness feels like time died
The power leaving your worries pacified
The magnetic pole where four seasons collide
And halfway between Earth and space.

The something you cannot replace
The six sparkling colors interlace
The air moves the rainbow apace
And what the future holds, no one knows.

The untold secrets of the land
The power in your idea's hand
The serenity of a place unmanned
And what the future holds, no one knows.

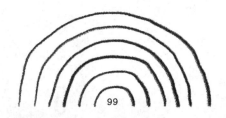

DRIPS & DROPS

Rapidly falling,
Racing from the *gray* above,
Hitting the <u>dry</u> ground,
Dripping and dropping—SPLASHES,
As it formed puddles and streams.

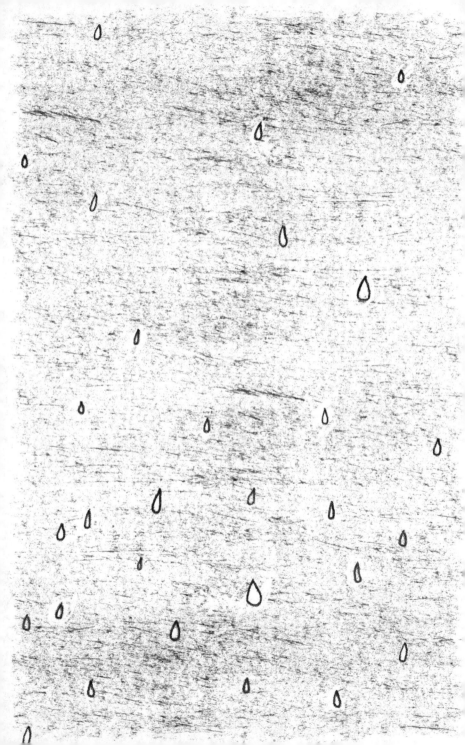

CROSSING TIGHTROPES

I'm quickly overwhelmed by the height
Flashing lights light my feet from below
I try to place each foot in the position that's right
And move step by step with flow.

The crowd cheers even louder
There's no going back
I'm running out of powder
As I look at the track.

The end is near
Though I start to tense
I shake with fear
It is so intense.

I step onto the platform and end in style
I have made it, with an even bigger smile.

The Candle Flame

The
candle
flame shines
brightly in the
dark. The smooth
flame will capture
your attention, steal
your focus, and calm you.
The bright hot colors
move back and
forth, burning softly. Aromas fill the
air, as the flame melts the wax of the
candle. The candle flame breathes in
surrounding oxygen, making the hot
flame grow in size. Close objects are
warmed by the candle flame. Surfaces
around the candle are splashed with
orange, as the flame burns eagerly
inside the glass. The flame, always
burning slightly and silently. The candle
flame burns and shines brightly in the dark.

Sea Mist

The waves swayed
In the breeze
Sea mist sprayed
My face with ease

Refreshing my thoughts
Changing my mood
The joy it brought
Left gratitude.

THINK

Do you often think about that dream life?
Do you think about that thought where you can rise?
Because if you were wise you would rise, up out of that
hole where followers lie, waiting for a leader to save the
world all in perfect time.
But that will never happen.
Because it's like we're in a World, where money is the
only compromise.
And every day innocence dies, and terrorists survive,
when they apologize.
And we could harmonize.
But we instead spend our days watching our own stealth
die,
through the wealth of our lies.

And maybe one day we'll come by, that thought where
we all gratify life.

But until then, let's all be depressed and cry, 'cause that's
the only thing we're doing, and it might only just get you
by.
But get with the times, the times are change. And strive
for change, where we can go that range and bring change
into our lives.

And to this day, we still can't all be equalized. And it's like the governments are advised, that extra millions will come their way, if the truth is continued to be disguised.

Stop hiding, and fight for your money, fight for your well-being, and fight for your rights.

Because life is for the living, so find some happiness, and start living your life.

THE CONTROLLING REMOTE

On the table it lays,
Changing channels when it likes.

The attitude it displays,
It annoys you when it strikes.

On and off the TV goes,
Without a person in sight.

It's strange when it changes TV shows,
Interrupting TV time, without an invite,

You just want to throw and squash it.
But you can't watch TV without it.

So, it's replaced straightaway!

MENTAL MARATHON

I went to bed with two bullet trains in my brain, one is ideas and the other one, thoughts. After days of writing, they rushed around crossing tracks, racing toward a finished product.

14th of November

The birds were singing,
The sun was bringing,
Happiness our way.

The day had departed,
But before I started,
I took a moment to lay.

After Lunch

There once was a massive blue plate,
with crumbs of a sandwich you ate,
and as it went down . . .
you gained a large frown . . .
because it did not taste too great.

LIVING IN LUGGAGE

The city streets, lots of feet, and rushing trains.
Tall old trees, the red sun's heat on the country plains.
Living in luggage
Opening doors, apartment floors, and different faces.
Arriving on diverse shores, brand-new stores, and
interesting places.
Travelling
Turning pages, performing on unusual stages, and
sighting flags.
Audience of different ages, contracts with varied wages,
and lots of jet lag.
Living in luggage
Every day is new, on my poetry pursuit, and a change has
wrought,
an amazing view, and I construe, lots of thoughts.
Travelling
Arrive and depart, leaving a part, that wasn't there
before.
Speaking art, from the center of my heart, with new
words to explore.
Living in luggage
Circling dates, interviews await, and rehearsals are go.
I don't hesitate, to create, rhythm and flow.
Travelling
I return home, only to roam, and travel ranges.
Like in a tome, the waves continue to foam, and poetry
continues to unravel changes.
Living in luggage.

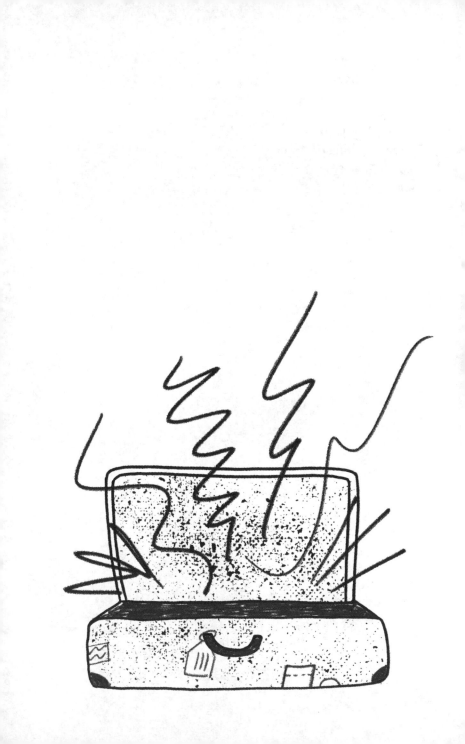

Snow

Elegantly cold
Icy air racing past you
Infinite magic.

THE PLACES YOU CAN GO
WITH ONE IDEA

The places you can go with one idea,
The opening of a new door arises
When you let your creativity steer.

Becoming a pioneer to persevere
Reaching for the stars, as the sun rises
The places you can go with one idea.

Everything comes from nothing, only without fear.
When your heart improvises
When you let your creativity steer.

To keep going, even when the end is near
And the things you learn when someone apprises
The places you can go with one idea.

From the saying, "blood, sweat, and tears."
You can stay strong, when life destabilizes
When you let your creativity steer.

Nothing will interfere.
When your imagination summarizes
The places you can go with one idea,
When you let your creativity steer.

ABOUT the AUTHOR

At twelve, Solli Raphael is the youngest winner of the Australian Poetry Slam held at the Sydney Opera House annually.

A budding humanitarian, he hopes to become an inspirational leader among his peers. Solli enjoys writing powerful and emotive poetry and performing pieces to instigate change in the areas he feels are critical for attention and action such as social equality, the environment, and animal protection.

Now thirteen, Solli is keen to use the platforms of performing and writing to tackle current social issues—big and small. As a voice of his generation, and at a time when youth movements worldwide hold much importance, his first extraordinary book, *Limelight*, showcases creativity and the power of social consciousness.

ACKNOWLEDGMENTS

I would like to thank my mum for her endless hours of hard work and help with setting up my business and being my manager, for supporting me in the pursuit of my dreams, and for just being a great mum.

Thank you to my family and friends who have been so helpful during my journey of becoming a young entrepreneur and in helping me to spread the messages that I write about in my poetry. Everyone's support, both online and in the "real" world, has really meant a lot to me.

I appreciate all of the recent performance opportunities too: APS, XXI Commonwealth Games, and TEDxSydney 2018.

Oh, and a last thank you to Jess Owen, Lisa Riley, and the many other amazing people at Penguin Random House Australia. I really want to thank you for believing in me and my passion for writing and sharing my messages across the world.

~ Solli